Making Major Financial Decisions

SOUTH-WESTERN

MAKING MAJOR FINANCIAL DECISIONS

Ransbottom & Nichol

LuEllen Ransbottom
Former Instructor
Adult and Vocational Education
Ormond Beach, Florida

Fran Moreland Nichol
Freelance Writer
Decatur, Georgia

SOUTH-WESTERN PUBLISHING CO.

Developmental Editor: *Mark Linton*
Senior Production Editor: *Alan Biondi*
Associate Director/Design: *Darren Wright*
Associate Photo Editor/Stylist: *Linda Ellis*
Marketing Manager: *Shelly Battenfield*

ISBN: 0-538-70841-7

1 2 3 4 5 6 7 8 H 99 98 97 96 95 94 93 92

Printed in the United States of America

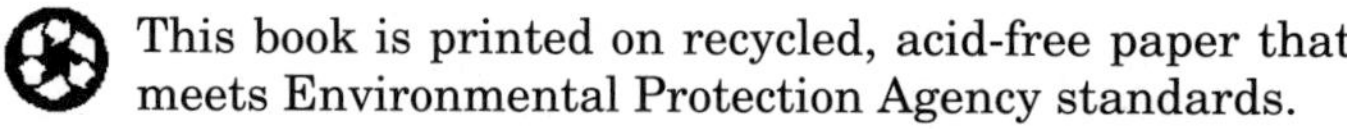
This book is printed on recycled, acid-free paper that meets Environmental Protection Agency standards.

PREFACE

Making Major Financial Decisions covers the skills needed for establishing credit, and for making decisions about housing and transportation. This text-workbook is written specifically for the adult learner and is designed to permit self-paced, individualized instruction and foster student success.

The main focus of ***Making Major Financial Decisions*** is on helping learners understand what wise choices are concerning credit, housing, and transportation. The advantages and disadvantages of credit are discussed, along with the responsibilities of landlords and tenants. Students learn how to complete a rental application and a lease agreement. Students learn to look at their transportation options, and they learn the information and skills needed when buying a used or new automobile.

SPECIAL FEATURES

Making Major Financial Decisions is designed to help adult learners develop the skills needed to establish credit and to make wise housing and transportation choices. Some features of the text-workbook include:

- A larger typeface is used to make the text-workbook easier for the student to read and use. Pages are colorful and uncrowded.
- Competency-based methodology is used. Clear objectives are presented followed by short segments of instruction. These are followed by student activities for immediate reinforcement.
- Content and examples relate to adult-level, real-life issues and skills.
- Pre- and post-tests, with answers and evaluation charts, are included for self-evaluation.
- Study breaks are included to provide refreshing and useful information that contributes to the general literacy of the student.
- Abundant exercises are included, each designed so that the student experiences frequent and meaningful success.
- Goals are listed for each exercise to provide motivation and direction.
- All exercises are supported with Bonus Exercises for the student who needs a second chance to succeed.

- Answers to all exercises are included to facilitate independent, self-paced learning.
- Personal progress is recorded by the student after completing each exercise.
- Individual success is measured by evaluation guides in the student's Personal Progress Record.

INSTRUCTOR'S MANUAL

The Instructor's Manual provides instructional strategies and specific teaching suggestions for ***Making Major Financial Decisions,*** along with supplementary bonus exercises and answers, additional testing materials, and a certificate of completion.

Bonus Exercises. A bonus exercise, matching each exercise in the text-workbook, is provided in the manual. These bonus exercises make it possible for students to have a second chance to reach the goals set for each exercise. Answers to the bonus exercises are also provided in the manual. These materials may be reproduced for classroom use.

Testing Materials. Two additional tests, with answers, are provided in the manual to allow for more flexible instruction and evaluation.

Certificate of Completion. Upon completion of ***Making Major Financial Decisions,*** a student's success may be recognized through a certificate of completion. This certificate lists the skills and topics covered in this text-workbook. A certificate master is included in the manual.

CONTENTS

GETTING ACQUAINTED

All of us have to make major financial decisions. We may or may not use personal credit. But we all have to make decisions about where we live and what kind of transportation we use. This book will help you with those decisions.

You will learn how to establish credit and what some of the advantages and disadvantages of credit are. You will learn your credit rights. You will learn how to make the best choices for housing and transportation.

Before you begin, meet the Valentine family. Rose Anna and Tony Valentine have had some rough times, but they are learning to manage their lives better. Rose Anna and Tony have two children, Buster, six, and Tisha, still in diapers. As you go through this book, Rose Anna and Tony will be learning about making major financial decisions with you. When you finish, all of you will have the skills you need to make these decisions.

HOW YOU WILL LEARN

Making Major Financial Decisions is written with you in mind. You will learn skills that can help you right away. This book begins with the information and skills you need for establishing credit, and it continues with useful studies about making housing and transportation decisions.

Learn at Your Own Pace

You will progress through the lessons in this book at your own pace. You may move ahead faster, or go slower, than other students. But don't be concerned about this. You are to work at *your* best speed.

Learn Skills Successfully

You are given objectives and goals for each unit. You will know what you are to accomplish. You will study a topic. Then you will complete an exercise. This lets you drill over what you have just learned. When you have shown that you know the topic, you will move on to the next topic. You will always know just how well you are doing as you move through each step in this book.

Complete Bonus Exercises

You may not reach your goal on every practice exercise. When this happens, you should review the lesson and then complete a Bonus Exercise. These exercises cover the same lessons as the practice exercises in this book. They give you a second chance to reach your goal. When you score higher on a Bonus Exercise than you did on the original activity, you may change your score on your Personal Progress Record. Your instructor has copies of these Bonus Exercises and the answers to them.

Check Your Own Success

You will keep track of your own success. You will check all of your own work. The answers are in the back of this book. The color pages make them easy to find. Always do the exercises *before* you look at the answers. Use the answers as a tool to verify your work —not as a means of filling in the blanks. You will record your scores on your own Personal Progress Record, which is also in the back of this book.

WHAT YOU WILL LEARN

As you study this book, you will learn how to establish credit and how to make the best decisions about housing and transportation choices.

In Unit 1, "Understanding Credit," you will learn the advantages and disadvantages of using credit. You will learn the major laws that protect your credit rights and how to prepare a loan application.

In Unit 2, "Understanding Housing Choices," you will learn how to make housing choices and how to find rental property. You will learn the responsibilities of landlords and tenants. You will learn how to complete a rental application and a lease agreement.

In Unit 3, "Buying Transportation," you will learn some of the terms used in buying and selling cars. You will learn the costs of owning a new car and the skills needed in buying a car, whether new or used.

SPECIAL FEATURES

Making Major Financial Decisions has a number of special features. These features will help you learn and apply the material successfully.

Checking What You Know

You can check what you already know about making major financial decisions before you start studying this book. *Checking What You Know* lets you know what skills you need to improve upon. Then, when you complete this book, you will do an exercise called *Checking What You Have Learned.* By comparing these two scores you will see how much you have gained through your study.

Making Your Money Work for You

This book has special features designed to give you a break from the regular study. These breaks have interesting stories about your money and helpful hints for making your money work for you.

Putting It Together

Each unit has a number of short exercises called *Checkpoints.* These exercises will help you check your understanding of a specific topic before continuing. At the end of each unit you will find a section titled *Putting It Together.* This section contains several exercises that are similar to the Checkpoints. They will help you to reinforce the skills you learned in each unit.

Personal Progress Record

You will keep track of your own progress. Once you check your answers, you will record your score on your *Personal Progress Record* at the end of this book. After you finish a unit, you will be able to see your level of success.

Completion Certificate

When you finish your study in this book you may be eligible for a certificate of completion. Your instructor will explain to you the skill level required for this award.

READY TO START

You are now ready to start learning about making major financial decisions. The skills you will learn in this book are skills you can use right away.

Turn to page xiii and complete Checking What You Know. Check your answers with the answers on page 53. Then begin Unit 1, "Understanding Credit."

LuEllen Ransbottom
Fran Moreland Nichol

CHECKING WHAT YOU KNOW

Take this pre-test before starting *Making Major Financial Decisions.* The 20 questions will tell you how much you already know about making decisions about major financial matters. They will also tell you what you need to learn.

There is no time limit, so take your time. When you finish, check your answers. Give yourself 1 point for each correct answer. Record you score on your Personal Progress Record. After finishing the book, you will be able to see how much you learned.

DIRECTIONS: Each statement is either true or false. Write *T* (true) or *F* (false) in the space provided.

______ 1. Using credit is buying something now and agreeing to pay for it later.

______ 2. Major purchases like cars and houses almost always require the use of credit.

______ 3. It is not wise to use credit to purchase durable items.

______ 4. A disadvantage of credit is that it limits what and when you can purchase items.

______ 5. Before you can be given credit, the lender must determine that you are a good credit risk.

______ 6. When applying for credit, you will have to furnish the names of your present and past employees.

______ 7. The Equal Credit Opportunity Act protects you against fraud.

______ 8. The biggest expense most people have is housing.

______ 9. A studio apartment consists of one large room that serves as kitchen, living room, and bedroom.

______ 10. The person who owns the property and receives rent is the landlord or lessor.

______ 11. The legal proceeding by which a landlord can force a tenant to move out is called a warrant.

______ 12. The landlord is responsible for providing heat during cold weather months.

______ 13. The landlord is responsible for removing garbage from the apartment or house.

______ 14. Rental applications usually require both personal and credit references.

______ 15. Walking and bicycling are the two most popular forms of transportation.

______ 16. Most people who buy a car must finance the purchase price.

______ 17. Car insurance usually costs more if you live in a rural area.

______ 18. Gas and oil will be a regular expense if you own a car.

______ 19. If you know what to look for in a car, private sellers can be your best source for a used car.

______ 20. Always test drive a car before you buy.

☞ ***Check Your work on page 53. Record your score on page 55.***

UNIT 1 Understanding Credit

WHAT YOU WILL LEARN

When you finish this unit, you will be able to:

- List five steps to follow in establishing credit.
- List five rules to follow when using credit.
- Calculate the cost of credit.
- Identify three laws that protect credit users.
- List five things to do if you are refused credit.
- Prepare a credit loan application.

Rose Anna Valentine's refrigerator quit working today. After a phone call, she found out that repairing it would cost more than it was worth. So, Rose Anna studied her budget to see what she could afford.

Rose Anna decided that she could afford a new refrigerator if she could make low monthly payments. But she did not have credit established. "My friend Joanna just bought a TV on credit from A-1 Appliances," she thought. "I'll go there to buy my refrigerator on credit." Rose Anna quickly found out that there is a lot to know about using credit.

ESTABLISHING CREDIT

Credit is buying something now and agreeing to pay for it later. Credit also means borrowing money and agreeing to pay it back later.

Major purchases like cars and houses almost always require the use of credit. Credit can also be useful in other ways. A good credit record can help when you rent an apartment or apply for services such as telephone, electricity, or cable TV. Credit cards can also eliminate the need for carrying large amounts of cash.

Credit should be used wisely. It is wise to use credit for buying a home, car, or major appliance. You should not use credit for perishable purchases. **Perishable purchases** are items that are used up soon after purchase. Examples of perishable purchases are meals, groceries, gas, or airline tickets.

Advantages of Using Credit

Credit allows you to buy an item when you need it but do not have cash. You can use credit to pay for something over a period of time. Credit also lets you take advantage of sales and meet emergencies.

Disadvantages of Using Credit

Credit can lead you to spend more than you can afford. Credit also adds to the cost of an item. Other disadvantages of using credit are that it can:

- Tempt you to buy items you do not need.
- Reduce the amount of comparative shopping you do.
- Tie up future income.

How to Qualify for Credit

You cannot walk into your local store or lending agency and expect to be given credit. You must first show the lender that you are a good credit risk. **Risk** is the chance the lender takes as to whether you will pay what you owe.

Before deciding whether or not you are a good risk, the lender is entitled to information about your character, capacity, and capital. *Character* refers to your reputation. It includes how honest, dependable, and mature you are. *Capacity* refers to your ability to make payments on your account. It includes information about your job, how much money you make, and what you owe. *Capital* refers to what you own.

Steps to Follow in Establishing Credit

Before you need credit, prepare for using credit. Creditors and lenders want to know how you handle responsibility. Follow these steps to establish credit.

Illustration 1-1

Credit allows people to buy when they do not have cash, but it can lead to spending more than they can afford.

1. Maintain a permanent residence. You will not be considered a good credit risk if you move often or have a bad record as a tenant. Your landlord may be asked about you.
2. Have a steady job. It will be easier to get credit if you have a record of working regularly.
3. Open a checking or savings account. A bank is a good credit reference.
4. Pay bills on time. Before granting credit, most companies will check to see if you pay electric, gas, and telephone bills on time. If you have a record of late payments, you will not be considered a good credit risk.
5. Establish credit with a local department store by making a small installment purchase and paying it promptly.
6. Take a small loan from your bank and repay it promptly. This gives you a credit record.
7. Apply for bank, gasoline, or department store credit cards. These are often easy to obtain. They will work best for you if you have little or no money owed.

CHECKPOINT 1-1

YOUR GOAL: Get 5 or more points.

Read carefully the statements below. Complete the statements by filling in the spaces provided. Use the words from the list below. An example is done for you.

- *Perishable purchases* are items that are used up soon after purchase.

1. It is not wise to use credit to purchase ____________ or ____________.
2. ____________ is buying something now and agreeing to pay for it later.
3. Before applying for credit you should maintain a ____________.
4. If you have a record of late payments for gas and electric bills, you will be considered a poor ____________.
5. It is wise to use credit when buying a ____________ or a ____________.

credit risk	**home**
perishable purchases	**groceries**
gas	**car**
credit	**permanent residence**

☞ *Check your work on page 53. Record your score on page 56.*

Rules to Follow When Using Credit

Credit is a way to have the things you need while you are still paying for them. But credit can also cause you trouble. Here are some rules to follow when you use credit:

1. Never sign a blank loan or installment contract. A **contract** is an agreement between two parties. Never sign an agreement unless everything is clearly written before you sign.
2. Keep your total debt at less than 20 percent of your after-tax income. Your **after-tax income** is your total income minus social security and income taxes. If your annual after-tax

income is $10,000, your total debt should not exceed $2,000. Total debt includes all credit card and loan contracts.

3. Never have more debt than you could pay off completely with 12 months of your present income.
4. Avoid using your savings to pay monthly bills. You should be able to pay monthly bills, credit cards, and installment loans without using your savings.
5. Always make monthly payments. Keep all debt low enough to make payments every month.
6. Avoid cosigning a loan. To **cosign** is to promise to repay a loan if the borrower does not. If the borrower does not repay the loan, you will be responsible for the entire remaining balance.
7. Never borrow from a small loan company to pay other bills. Small loan companies advertise consolidation loans. A consolidation loan is a loan used to pay off two or more other debts. Consolidation loans can lead to all of the disadvantages of using credit.
8. Keep your credit account balances low. You can get in trouble very quickly by allowing balances to increase for several months. If your balance increases one month, do not charge anything else until you pay it down.

Kinds of Credit

There are many kinds of credit available. The most commonly used sources of credit are:

Banks

Banks make many kinds of loans. One of the most common kinds of bank loan is the installment loan. An **installment loan,** or installment purchase agreement, is a contract in which the total purchase price and credit cost is divided into equal amounts for repayment. Often the bank has the right to take the property you bought with borrowed money if you do not repay the loan.

Bank Cards

Bank cards are also commonly called *credit cards*. A **bank card** is a credit agreement through which you can continue to charge purchases even though you have not paid the account in full. VISA and MasterCard are examples of bank or credit cards. Banks will set a limit on the amount you can charge. Interest will be charged on the unpaid balance. There is also usually an annual fee.

Charge Accounts

A **charge account** is credit for merchandise given by a store. The store will send a bill each month. Interest will be charged on the unpaid balance.

Finance Companies

Finance companies charge higher rates because they loan money to many people who are higher risk.

Pawnshops

A **pawnshop** is a shop that lends money in exchange for personal property left at the shop. If the loan is not repaid, the borrower forfeits the property.

Lay-Away

Lay-away plans allow buyers to put aside an item until it is paid for in full. Most lay-away plans have a service fee of up to 5 percent of the value of the item.

CHECKPOINT 1-2

YOUR GOAL: Get 4 or more points.

Read carefully the statements below. Each statement is either true or false. Write *T* (true) or *F* (false) beside each statement in the space provided. An example is done for you.

__F__ • It is all right to sign a blank loan contract.

_____ 1. Total debt should not exceed 20 percent of your after-tax income.

_____ 2. Charge accounts do not charge interest on the unpaid balance.

_____ 3. Savings should be used to pay overdue monthly bills.

_____ 4. When you cosign a loan, you are responsible for the entire unpaid balance if the borrower does not pay.

_____ 5. Small loan companies are good sources of loans.

☞ ***Check your work on page 53. Record your score on page 56.***

The Cost of Credit

Credit is not free. Before using credit, you need to find out what it will cost you. In some cases, you are given a cash price and a credit price. To find the cost of credit, subtract the cash price from the credit price. For example:

Credit price......	$388.00
Cash price........	-300.00
Cost of credit....	$ 88.00

Sometimes you will have only the down payment and monthly payments for an item you want to buy. You can still find out the cost of credit. For example, you may be looking at a $300 videocassette recorder. The cash price of the recorder is $300. You can buy it for $100 down and 12 monthly payments of $24.00 each. To find the total cost, first multiply the *amount* of payments times the *number* of payments:

Amount of payments......	$ 24.00
Number of payments.....	x 12
Total...............................	$288.00

Add the down payment to get the total you will pay:

Total of 12 payments....	$288.00
Down payment.............	+100.00
Total............................	$388.00

That's the total you will pay. Now subtract the cash price from the credit price to find out how much you are paying for the use of credit:

Credit price..........	$388.00
Cash price............	-300.00
Cost of credit........	$ 88.00

The cost of credit is usually a set amount called a *service charge*, or *interest*. **Interest** is the amount paid for the use of capital. Interest is usually expressed by a percentage of the amount you borrow. For example, you could borrow $100.00 for one year and pay interest at the rate of 10 percent. The dollar amount of interest would be $10 ($100 x .10 = $10.00). The rate of interest charged on most credit cards and installment loans is shown by the number called the *annual percentage rate* (APR). The higher the number, the more you are paying for credit.

UNDERSTANDING YOUR CREDIT RIGHTS

Credit is a privilege, not a right. You do not automatically have the right to use credit. You must earn that privilege.

There are, however, certain rights relating to credit that are protected by federal and state laws. These laws make sure you are treated fairly when you apply for credit. You also are protected against unfair billing or unfair collection practices, or credit costs that are too high. Some of these laws include the Equal Credit Opportunity Act, the Fair Credit Reporting Act, the Fair Credit Billing Act, and the Truth in Lending Act.

Equal Credit Opportunity Act

The Equal Credit Opportunity Act protects you against discrimination. **Discrimination** is the act of showing different favor or treatment on the basis of reasons other than individual merit. You cannot be denied credit because of your sex, race, religion, color, marital status, or age (except where your age affects your ability to complete the credit agreement). You cannot be denied credit because you receive unemployment, social security, retirement, or other benefits.

The Equal Credit Opportunity Act includes other statements about your credit rights. It is a Federal law. Many states also have similar laws; some of them are stricter than the Federal law.

Fair Credit Reporting Act

Credit reports contain information about you and your credit record. A **credit report** is a written report issued by a credit bureau. Under the Fair Credit Reporting Act you have the right to know what is in your credit report file. You also have the right to know who has seen your file.

Fair Credit Billing Act

Under the Fair Credit Billing Act creditors must correct errors within a specified time. You may get a bill for an item you did not purchase or you may get a bill for an item you returned. Once you notify the creditor about the error, the Fair Credit Billing Act requires that the correction be made promptly.

You are responsible for notifying your creditor if you find an error. Under the law, you must follow certain steps. These steps include:

1. Write the creditor within 60 days of getting the bill. Do not write on the bill. Use a separate sheet of paper. Include your

name, address, and account number. Give the dollar amount involved and explain why you believe it is an error.

2. Make sure you send the letter to the right address. Often this address is listed on the bill under *Send inquiries to.*
3. The creditor is required to acknowledge your letter within 30 days of receiving it. The creditor is also required to investigate the matter. The creditor must either correct the mistake or explain why the bill is correct.

The creditor cannot close your account just because you disputed a bill. You can get additional information about this and other credit laws by writing the Federal Trade Commission, Washington, DC 20580 and asking for a free brochure.

MAKING YOUR MONEY WORK FOR YOU

Under the Credit Card Regulations law, you must be sent a self-addressed, postage-paid envelope or post card for use in reporting a lost or stolen credit card. You should receive this with your credit card. If your card is lost or stolen, your maximum liability is $50.00. But you should report the loss or theft immediately. If it is reported before the card is used by an unauthorized person, you have no liability.

Truth in Lending Act

The Consumer Credit Protection Act of 1968, known as the Truth in Lending Act, requires that consumers be fully informed about credit costs before a purchase agreement is signed. Some of the information the creditor must give you, in writing, includes:

1. Cash price.
2. Down payment or trade-in amount or both.
3. Amount financed.
4. Insurance costs, filing costs, and any other miscellaneous costs.
5. Finance charge.
6. Annual percentage rate of the finance charge.

Under the Truth in Lending Act you are also given three business days in which to change your mind about a purchase. You cannot be penalized for changing your mind within this time.

What to Do If You Are Refused Credit

There are also laws to protect you from being unfairly refused credit. You can be refused credit if you have a bad credit record or if you are a poor credit risk. But the law protects you from unfair treatment. The creditor must either tell you why credit was refused or tell you of your right to know the reason. Here are steps to take if you are refused credit:

1. Find out the specific reason for which you were refused.
2. If you were refused on the basis of information in a credit bureau report, contact that credit bureau to find out if the information is correct.
3. If you find incorrect information, ask that it be corrected and that a corrected copy of your report be sent to the creditor.
4. If the problem results from too few satisfactory credit references being in your file, make sure all of your references have been reported to that particular credit bureau.
5. Make sure all satisfactory information has been reported to the creditor.
6. If you feel you have been denied credit in violation of the Equal Credit Opportunity Act (because of race, sex, or other discrimination), contact an attorney or an appropriate government agency.
7. If you are still denied credit, go to another creditor.

CHECKPOINT 1-3

YOUR GOAL: Get 4 or more points.

Read the words and phrases that follow. Each word or phrase is completed with one of the phrases listed after number 5. Put the correct answer (give the letter) in the answer blank that is before each word or phrase. An example is done for you.

_d_ • Equal Credit Opportunity Act

_____ 1. Fair Credit Billing Act

_____ 2. Truth in Lending Act

_____ 3. A creditor

______ 4. Credit laws

______ 5. Fair Credit Opportunity Act

a. Requires that creditors correct errors within a specified time.

b. Cannot close your account because you dispute a bill.

c. Guarantees your right to know what is in your credit report and who has seen it.

d. Protects you against discrimination when you apply for credit.

e. Requires that the consumer be fully informed about credit costs before an agreement is signed.

f. Require that the creditor tell you why you are refused credit.

☞ ***Check your work on page 53. Record your score on page 56.***

PREPARING A LOAN APPLICATION

Before you apply for credit, make sure you have the information you need. A credit officer will usually fill out the form for you. Many of the questions will be easy to answer. You should also have the following information:

1. Employment information:
   a. The date you began work for your present employer.
   b. The name and business address of your supervisor.
   c. Your monthly income.
2. Residence information:
   a. The address where you last lived.
   b. The name of your present and previous landlords.
3. Automobile information:
   a. Make, year, and tag number of your car if you own one.
   b. Name and address of your car finance company.
   c. Monthly payments and total amount left to be paid on the loan.
4. Other credit accounts:
   a. Creditor.
   b. Account number.
   c. Address.
   d. Monthly payments.
   e. Balance owing.

Rose Anna needed to buy a new refrigerator right away. She did not have the cash. So she applied for a loan from A-1 Appliance Store to purchase a refrigerator. Rose Anna's loan application is shown below, in Illustration 1-2.

THIS FORM MUST BE FILLED OUT COMPLETELY IN INK FOR CREDIT COMMITTEE ACTION.

APPLICATION FOR LOAN

I hereby apply for a loan in the amount of $ 500. repayable in 12 months

1. Computer No. LA 749
2. Soc. Sec. No. 437-00-2111

I DESIRE THE LOAN FOR THE FOLLOWING PURPOSE:				
Purchase refrigerator				
FIRST NAME: Rose		MIDDLE NAME: Anna		LAST NAME: Valentine
WORK TELEPHONE / LOCATION: 255-9111	POSITION: Clerk	SUPERVISOR: Wilson	EMPLOYMENT DATE: 6-14-89	INCOME: $ 950 /MO
RESIDENCE ADDRESS: 1765 Sheridan Dr.,	CITY: Ormond	STATE: Beach, FL		ZIP CODE: 32174
LAST PREVIOUS ADDRESS: 712 Circle Oak Ave.,	CITY: Daytona	STATE: Beach, FL		YEARS THERE: 4
BIRTHDATE: 7-14-76	TELEPHONE NUMBER: 672-5353		AGES OF DEPENDENTS: 6 years; 20 months	
NAME OF NEAREST RELATIVE NOT LIVING WITH YOU: Benita Sanchez,	COMPLETE ADDRESS: 712 Circle Oak Ave., Daytona Bch.		TELEPHONE NO.: 252-1312	RELATIONSHIP: Mother
HOME: ☐ OWN ☒ RENT	YEARS THERE: 2	MONTHLY MORTGAGE OR RENT PAYMENTS: $300.00	Home Financed By or Landlord Name: Village Apartments	

STATEMENT OF TOTAL INDEBTEDNESS AND LIABILITIES I am indebted to the following creditors (list all debts such as doctor bills, installments, loans, real estate mortgages, credit cards, etc. Attach additional sheet if necessary):

MAKE OF AUTO	YEAR	TAG #	IF FINANCED, BY WHOM	BALANCE OWING	MO. PAYMENTS
1. None					
2.					

NAME AND ACCOUNT NUMBER	ADDRESS	PURPOSE	BALANCE OWING	MO. PAYMENTS
None				

ARE YOU OBLIGATED TO MAKE ALIMONY / CHILD SUPPORT PAYMENTS? ☐ YES ☒ NO IF YES, HOW MUCH PER MONTH?

Illustration 1-2

Rose Anna's Loan Application

CHECKPOINT 1-4

YOUR GOAL: Get 4 or more points.

Read carefully the statements given at the top of the next page. Complete each statement by filling in the space provided. Use the list of words that follows. An example is done for you.

When you make application for a loan, you will need the following:

- The *tag number* of your car, if you own one.

1. The ________________ on any credit cards.
2. The name of your present and previous ________________.
3. The ________________ and ________________ of your job supervisor.
4. The name and address of your car ________________.
5. The ________________ on which you began your present job.

name
date
balance owing
tag number
landlords
finance company
business address

☞ *Check your work on page 53. Record your score on page 56.*

WHAT YOU HAVE LEARNED

After studying this unit you have learned:

- Five steps to follow in establishing credit.
- Five rules to follow when using credit.
- To calculate the cost of credit.
- Three laws that protect credit users.
- Five things to do if you are refused credit.
- To prepare a credit loan application.

ACTIVITY 1-1 YOUR GOAL: Get 10 or more points.

Complete the sample loan application below by writing in your own information in the spaces provided. The computer number and the amount and time of the loan are done for you.

THIS FORM MUST BE FILLED OUT COMPLETELY IN INK FOR CREDIT COMMITTEE ACTION.

APPLICATION FOR LOAN

I hereby apply for a loan in the amount of $ 500.00 repayable in 12 months

1. Computer No. LA749
2. Soc. Sec. No. ____________

I DESIRE THE LOAN FOR THE FOLLOWING PURPOSE:				
FIRST NAME		MIDDLE NAME		LAST NAME
WORK TELEPHONE / LOCATION	POSITION	SUPERVISOR	EMPLOYMENT DATE	INCOME $ /MO
RESIDENCE ADDRESS	CITY	STATE		ZIP CODE
LAST PREVIOUS ADDRESS	CITY	STATE		YEARS THERE
BIRTHDATE	TELEPHONE NUMBER		AGES OF DEPENDENTS	
NAME OF NEAREST RELATIVE NOT LIVING WITH YOU	COMPLETE ADDRESS		TELEPHONE NO.	RELATIONSHIP
HOME ☐ OWN ☐ RENT	YEARS THERE	MONTHLY MORTGAGE OR RENT PAYMENTS		Home Financed By or Landlord Name

STATEMENT OF TOTAL INDEBTEDNESS AND LIABILITIES I am indebted to the following creditors (list all debts such as doctor bills, installments, loans, real estate mortgages, credit cards, etc. Attach additional sheet if necessary):

MAKE OF AUTO	YEAR	TAG #	IF FINANCED, BY WHOM	BALANCE OWING	MO. PAYMENTS
1.					
2.					

NAME AND ACCOUNT NUMBER	ADDRESS	PURPOSE	BALANCE OWING	MO. PAYMENTS

ARE YOU OBLIGATED TO MAKE ALIMONY / CHILD SUPPORT PAYMENTS? ☐ YES ☐ NO IF YES, HOW MUCH PER MONTH?

☞ *Check your work on page 53. Record your score on page 56.*

ACTIVITY 1-2 YOUR GOAL: Get 8 or more points.

Match the numbered statements with the phrase listed below that best describes the statement. Write your answer in the space provided. An example is done for you.

__a__ • Credit allows you to buy an item when you need it but do not have the cash.

______ 1. Buying a car or major appliance.

______ 2. Pay bills on time.

______ 3. Keep your debts low enough to make payments every month.

______ 4. The difference between the credit price and the cash price.

______ 5. You cannot be denied credit because of your marital status.

______ 6. Credit can lead you to spend more than you can afford.

______ 7. Go to a restaurant for dinner and pay with a credit card.

______ 8. Have a steady job.

______ 9. Keep your total debt at less than 20 percent of your after-tax income.

______ 10. You are protected against unfair billing or collection practice.

a. Advantages of credit.
b. Wise Use of credit.
c. Disadvantages of credit.
d. Establishing credit.
e. Rules to follow when using credit.
f. Cost of credit.
g. Credit rights.
h. Unwise use of credit.

☞ ***Check your work on page 53. Record your score on page 56.***

UNIT 2

Understanding Housing Choices

WHAT YOU WILL LEARN

When you finish this unit, you will be able to:

- List three housing choices.
- Define six common terms used in rental property.
- List four ways to find rental property.
- List five things to look for when renting.
- List four responsibilities of a landlord.
- List four responsibilities of a tenant.
- Complete a rental application.
- Complete a lease agreement.

Things had changed with the Valentine family. Rose Anna and Tony were back together. Buster and Tisha thought that was fine, too. Tony's company had transferred him back to town, and he was getting a small raise.

With two incomes, they could afford a bigger place. Rose Anna and Tony wanted to make the right choice so they would get the most for their housing dollar. With Buster and Tisha as helpers, they began to look for a new home.

HOUSING CHOICES

Housing is the biggest expense most people have. Making the most of your housing dollar will help you manage your total budget. Choosing carefully and using wisely are the ways to keep housing costs low.

There are many different kinds of housing available. Most people spend more than half of their time at their home, so you will want to choose carefully.

Apartments

Apartments are usually the first choice when people move away from their parents. Apartments range in size from efficiency units to two-story townhouse units. An **efficiency apartment** (sometimes called a *studio apartment*) is a small apartment consisting of one large room that serves as kitchen, living room, and bedroom. A **townhouse** is a large apartment, usually two-story, with separate living and dining areas.

Apartments often offer facilities such as laundry rooms, storage areas, swimming pools, or playgrounds. They also often have rules about keeping pets, making noise, or hours for using the facilities.

Duplexes

A **duplex** is a two-family house. Both halves of a duplex are the same but each has a separate entrance. Duplexes may be upstairs and downstairs in one building or side by side. Duplexes offer more privacy than apartments and may have other advantages such as garages.

Duplexes often have more responsibilities, too. For example, if you rent a duplex, you may be required to mow the grass or trim the shrubs.

Houses

A **house** is a single-family home separate from other buildings. Buying a house is the biggest investment most families make. Rental houses may also offer good choices. Rental houses vary widely in price, size, and condition. Most owners of rental houses require the renter to maintain the yard.

Terms Used in Rental Property

Rental property is the most popular choice in housing. Renting usually costs less than buying. Renting also offers such advantages as convenience, social life, and mobility.

Some of the terms most commonly used in renting property include:

Illustration 2-1

Housing is the biggest expense most people have.

Landlord (Lessor) - The person owning the house or apartment you rent.
Tenant (Lessee) - Person renting the house or apartment.
Rent - Payment for use of property. Rent is usually paid monthly.
Lease - Legal agreement between landlord and tenant listing all obligations and requirements of occupancy.
Eviction - Legal proceeding by which a landlord can force a tenant to move out.
Security Deposit - Money deposited by a tenant in advance on a rental agreement. The money is held as *security* against any damage that may be caused by the tenant.
Forfeiture - Giving up your security deposit when you fail to meet obligations of the lease.
Housing Authority - City or county agency set up to uphold building and housing codes.
Sublet - To rent your apartment or house to someone else while you continue to pay the landlord.

CHECKPOINT 2-1

YOUR GOAL: Get 4 or more points.

Read carefully the statements on the next page. Complete each statement by filling in a word or words in the space provided. Use words from the list that follows. An example is done for you.

- A ___duplex___ is a two-family house.

1. Rental payment is usually made on a ______________________ basis.
2. An ______________________ apartment consists of one large room that serves as kitchen, living room, and bedroom.
3. The person owning the apartment you rent is called the ______________________ or ______________________.
4. A large, two-story apartment is often called a ______________________.
5. The ______________________ is the city or county agency set up to uphold building and housing codes.
6. The legal proceeding by which a landlord can force a tenant to move out is called ______________________.

landlord
efficiency
monthly
townhouse
duplex
eviction
housing authority
lessor

☞ *Check your work on page 53. Record your score on page 56.*

MAKING YOUR MONEY WORK FOR YOU

One way to cut your housing costs is through shared housing. You may have a friend or family member with whom you could share. If so, consider getting one larger place and dividing the costs. Make sure you have agreements in writing about paying bills, using facilities, and dividing responsibilities.

FINDING RENTAL PROPERTY

Look carefully for rental property. Ask friends and relatives about places they know. Read ads in local newspapers. You may also want to contact your local Housing Authority or a real estate agent. When you talk with agents, make sure their fees will be paid by the property owner, not by you.

Consider your needs in relation to the rental property. Location, size, cost, condition, and pets must be right for you. If not, you will be unhappy and soon looking for a new place to live.

1. *Location*. Make sure the property you choose is convenient to work, schools, and shopping. If you will be using public transportation, find out where the nearest transit stops are and how often trains or buses run.
2. *Size*. Look for how well you and your furnishings will fit. Look for closet and storage space. In apartment buildings, ask about additional storage areas.
3. *Cost*. Are gas, heat, and electricity included in the rent? If not, ask for recent bills showing the average monthly costs. You can often get these estimates from the utility company.

   Some states require that security deposits be put in a savings account and the interest paid to you annually. Find out if your deposit is refundable and under what conditions. How long will it take to get it back when you move? Ask who pays for maintenance of the property.
4. *Condition*. Are repairs needed? Will the landlord repaint before you move in? Make sure these things are done, or get a written agreement that they will be done within a certain time. Is the property damaged in any way? If so, make a list of damages and have the landlord sign it so you cannot be held responsible.
5. *Other questions*. If you have a pet, will you be allowed to keep it on the property? Will you be allowed to sublet?

RESPONSIBILITIES OF LANDLORDS AND TENANTS

All states have laws that protect both landlord and tenant. These laws vary from state to state. In general, the following rights and responsibilities exist.

Responsibilities of the Landlord

The landlord must obey all building, housing, and health codes that apply. If there are no local codes, the landlord is still responsible for keeping the property in reasonable condition, keeping the property safe, and keeping the plumbing in working order. Other responsibilities of the landlord include:

1. Extermination of rats, mice, and roaches.
2. Furnishing adequate locks and keys.
3. Keeping common areas clean and safe. Common areas are used by yourself as well as other people. For example, in an apartment complex, the grounds, parking lot, laundry room, and pool are common areas.
4. Providing outside garbage containers and making sure garbage and trash are regularly removed.
5. Providing heat during cold weather months.
6. Providing hot and cold running water.

Responsibilities of the Tenant

While living in the property, the tenant also has responsibilities. The tenant is expected to conduct himself or herself in a way that does not disturb neighbors or damage the property. Other responsibilities include:

1. Keeping the property clean and safe.
2. Removing garbage in a sanitary manner.
3. Maintaining plumbing fixtures. (The tenant should notify the landlord of major plumbing repairs needed.)
4. Using electrical, plumbing, heating, and other systems in a safe and reasonable manner.
5. Preventing destruction of or damage to the property.
6. Complying with all building, housing, or health codes that apply to tenants.

CHECKPOINT 2-2

YOUR GOAL: Get 6 or more points.

Read carefully the statements below. Each statement is either true or false. Write *T* (true) or *F* (false) beside each statement in the space provided. An example is done for you.

___*T*___ • Size and location should be considered when looking for rental property.

______ 1. It is not necessary to ask about security deposits before signing a rental agreement.

______ 2. Landlords will always complete repairs needed before a new tenant moves into their property.

______ 3. Some landlords will not allow pets to be kept on their properties.

______ 4. Landlords are not responsible for furnishing locks and keys to their properties.

______ 5. Tenants must remove garbage in a sanitary manner.

______ 6. Landlords must provide hot and cold running water.

______ 7. Tenants must make all major plumbing repairs.

______ 8. Tenants are responsible for using plumbing, heating, and other systems in a safe and reasonable manner.

☞ *Check your work on page 53. Record your score on page 56.*

COMPLETING A RENTAL APPLICATION

Rental applications help the landlord know if you would be a good tenant. When you are completing a rental application, have all the information you will need in advance. Information needed includes:

1. Name, address, and telephone number of your employer.
2. Name, address, and telephone number of your spouse's employer.
3. Name and address of your present landlord.
4. Name, address, and telephone number of at least four references. A reference is someone who can verify what you say. You will need two kinds of references:

    a. Credit references, who can verify what you say about your financial responsibility. Your bank is a good credit reference. Charge card companies with whom you do business or stores where you are a regular customer are other credit references.

    b. Personal references, who can verify what you say about your character and conduct. Your minister or rabbi, your neighbors, or coworkers are good personal references.

Tony and Rose Anna wanted to rent a duplex on Main Street. The rental application they completed is shown in Illustration 2-2 at the top of the following page.

COMPLETING A LEASE AGREEMENT

A lease agreement should protect both you and the landlord. Before you sign a lease agreement, make sure it contains the following things:

1. The date on which the agreement takes effect.
2. The length of time that the agreement covers.

RENTAL APPLICATION

DATE October 5, 19--

APPLICANT (1) Rose Anna Valentine

APPLICANT (2) Tony Valentine

OCCUPANTS OTHER THAN APPLICANTS (CHILDREN'S NAMES & AGES) Buster, 6

Tisha, 2 OTHER None

NUMBER OF AUTOS YOU WOULD KEEP AT THIS ADDRESS 1 PETS 0

PRESENT HOME ADDRESS 1765 Sheridan Dr. Apt. 3 HOW LONG 3 years

PRESENT LANDLORD Village Apartments, Inc. ADDRESS 1700 Sheridan Drive

HOW LONG IN THIS CITY 15 years WHERE PREVIOUSLY 991 Quail Run

NAME AND ADDRESS TO BE NOTIFIED IN CASE OF EMERGENCY Bonita Sanchez

712 Circle Oak Ave, Daytona Beach, Fl. PHONE 555-1321

EMPLOYER (1) Discount Mart HOW LONG 3 years

ADDRESS 2602 E. 10th Street, Ormond Beach PHONE 555-9111

EMPLOYER (2) Townsend Industries HOW LONG 2 years

ADDRESS 471 S. Nova Road, Ormond Beach PHONE 555-3214

REFERENCES

CREDIT REFERENCES	ADDRESS	PHONE
1. ABC Appliances Co.	500 Mason Ave.	555-7000
2. Apex Utilities Corp.	475 N. Atlantic Ave.	555-1201
3. U.S. Telephone Co.	795 S. Ridgewood Ave.	555-5000
PERSONAL REFERENCES	ADDRESS	PHONE
1. Silvia Brown	1769 Sheridan Dr., Apt. 1	555-9181
2. Manuel Cintron	110 Rio Pinar	555-1010
BANK: Security State Bank		

Illustration 2-2

Rose Anna and Tony's Rental Application

3. A full description of the property.
4. The amount of rental payment.
5. The date on which payment is due.
6. How and where rent is to be paid.
7. The amount of security deposit, if any.
8. Expenses that are included or not included (such as utilities, laundry facilities, master TV antenna, or storage space.)

9. Signatures of all parties.

A lease can also cover special circumstances. For example, if you know you will stay for several years, the lease should provide for renewal. The lease might also specify how much your rent can increase. Other considerations include:

1. If you move before your lease expires, will you be allowed to sublet?
2. If you have children, are they allowed?
3. Can you make changes to the property? You may want to paint or put up shelves. If so, the lease should spell out who will pay for such changes.

Tony and Rose Anna reached an agreement with Mrs. Munoz, the owner, for the Valentine family to move into the duplex on Main Street. The lease agreement they signed is shown on the following page in Illustration 2-3.

CHECKPOINT 2-3

YOUR GOAL: Get 4 or more points.

Read carefully the statements below. Some of the statements are true; some are false. Write a *T* beside each correct statement. Write an *F* beside each incorrect statement. Use the space provided. An example is done for you.

_F_ • A store where you have never shopped can be a credit reference for you.

_____ 1. A lease agreement is only for the protection of the landlord.

_____ 2. Your minister, rabbi, or neighbor can be a good personal reference.

_____ 3. All parties to the agreement must sign a lease.

_____ 4. If you have a baby after you move into an "Adults Only" apartment complex, you cannot be asked to move.

_____ 5. A lease agreement should list what expenses are included or not included, such as utilities and storage.

_____ 6. Rent can be paid within 60 days after the date due.

Check your work on page 53. Record your score on page 56.

RESIDENTIAL LEASE AGREEMENT
AND SECURITY DEPOSIT RECEIPT

THIS INDENTURE, made this 15th day of October, 19 --, between Maria Munoz, hereinafter designated the Lessor or Landlord, and Tony Valentine and Rose Anna Valentine, hereinafter designated the Lessee.

WITNESSETH: That the said Lessor/Landlord does by these presents lease and demise the residence situated at 1639 Main Street in Ormond Beach City, Volusia County, Florida State, of which the real estate is described as follows:

1639 Main Street, Ormond Beach, Florida

upon the following terms and conditions:

1. **Term:** The premises are leased for a term of one (1) years, commencing the 1st day of November, 19 --, and terminating the 31st day of October 19 --.

2. **Rent:** The Lessee shall pay rent in the amount of $ 400.00 per month for the above premises on the 1st day of each month in advance to Landlord.

3. **Utilities:** Lessee shall pay for service and utilities supplied to the premises, except city water which will be furnished by Landlord.

4. **Sublet:** The Lessee agrees not to sublet said premises nor to assign this agreement nor any part thereof without the prior written consent of Landlord.

5. **Inspection of Premises:** Lessee agrees that he has made inspection of the premises and accepts the condition of the premises in its present state, and that there are no repairs, changes, or modifications to said premises to be made by Landlord other than as listed herein.

6. **Lessee Agrees:**
(1) To keep said premises in a clean and sanitary condition;
(2) To properly dispose of rubbish, garbage and waste in a clean and sanitary manner at reasonable and regular intervals and to assume all costs of extermination and fumigation for infestation caused by Lessee;
(3) To properly use and operate all electrical, gas, heating, plumbing facilities, fixtures and appliances;
(4) To not intentionally or negligently destroy, deface, damage, impair or remove any part of the premises, their appurtenances, facilities, equipment, furniture, furnishings, and appliances, nor to permit any member of his family, invitee, licensee or other person acting under his control to do so;
(5) Not to permit a nuisance or common waste.

7. **Maintenance of Premises:** Lessee agrees to mow and water the grass and lawn, and keep the grass, lawn, flowers and shrubbery thereon in good order and condition, and keep the sidewalk surrounding said premises free and clear of all obstructions; to replace in a neat and workmanlike manner all glass and doors broken during occupancy thereof; to use due precaution against freezing of water or waste pipes and stoppage of same in and about said premises and that in case water or waste pipes are frozen or become clogged by reason of neglect of Lessee, the Lessee shall repair the same at his own expense as well as all damage caused thereby.

8. **Alterations:** Lessee agrees not to make alterations or do or cause to be done any painting or wallpapering to said premises without the prior written consent of Landlord.

9. **Use of Premises:** Lessee shall not use said premises for any purpose other than that of residence and shall not use said premises or any part thereof for ant illegal purpose. Lessee agrees to conform to municipal, county and state code, statutes, ordinances and regulations concerning the use and occupation of said premises.

10. **Pets and Animals:** Lessee shall not maintain any pets or animals upon the premises without the prior written consent of Landlord.

11. **Access:** Landlord shall have the right to place and maintain "for rent" signs in a conspicuous place on said premises for thirty days prior to the vacation of said premises. Landlord reserves the right of access to the premises for the purpose of:
(a) Inspection;
(b) Repairs, alterations or improvements;
(c) To supply services of; or
(d) To exhibit or display the premises to prospective or actual purchasers, mortgagees, tenants, workman, or contractors.
Access shall be at reasonable times except in case of emergency or abandonment.

12. **Surrender of Premises:** In the event of default in payment of any installation of rent or at the expiration of said term of this lease, Lessee will quit and surrender the said premises to Landlord.

13. **Security Deposit:** The Lessee has deposited the sum of $ 400.00 receipt of which is hereby acknowledged, which sum shall be deposited by Landlord in a trust account with Citizens bank; savings and loan association or licensed escrow, Granada branch, whose address is 14 East Granada Boulevard, Ormond Beach, FL 32174-4214.

All or a portion of such deposit may be retained by Landlord and a refund of any portion of such deposit is conditioned as follows:
(1) Lessee shall fully perform obligations hereunder and those pursuant to Chapter 207, Laws of 1973, 1st Ex Session or as may be subsequently amended;
(2) Lessee shall occupy said premises for one (1) months or longer from date hereof;
(3) Lessee shall clean and restore said residence and return the same to Landlord in its initial condition, except for reasonable wear and tear, upon the termination of this tenancy and vacation of apartment;
(4) Lessee shall have remedied or repaired any damage to apartment premises;
(5) Lessee shall surrender to Landlord the keys to premises;
Any refund from security deposit, as by itemized statement shown to be due to Lessee, shall be returned to Lessee within fourteen (14) days after termination of this tenancy and vacation of the premises.

IN WITNESS WHEREOF, the Lessee has hereunto set his hand and seal the day and year first above written.

Maria Munoz	Tony Valentine
LANDLORD	LESSEE
1641 Main Street	Rosa Anna Valentine
Ormond Beach, FL 32174-1232	LESSEE
ADDRESS	

Illustration 2-3

Tony and Rose Anna's Lease Agreement

WHAT YOU HAVE LEARNED

After studying this unit you have learned:

- Three housing choices.
- Six common terms used in rental property.
- Four ways to find rental property.
- Five things to look for when renting.
- Four responsibilities of a landlord.
- Four responsibilities of a tenant.
- How to complete a rental application.
- How to complete a lease agreement.

ACTIVITY 2-1

YOUR GOAL: Get 5 or more points.

Complete the following Rental Application using your own information as though you are Applicant (1).

RENTAL APPLICATION

DATE ____________________

APPLICANT (1) ____________________

APPLICANT (2) ____________________

OCCUPANTS OTHER THAN APPLICANTS (CHILDREN'S NAMES & AGES) ____________________

____________________ OTHER ____________________

NUMBER OF AUTOS YOU WOULD KEEP AT THIS ADDRESS ____________ PETS ________

PRESENT HOME ADDRESS ____________________ HOW LONG ____________

PRESENT LANDLORD ____________ ADDRESS ____________________

HOW LONG IN THIS CITY ____________ WHERE PREVIOUSLY ____________________

NAME AND ADDRESS TO BE NOTIFIED IN CASE OF EMERGENCY ____________________

____________________ PHONE ____________

EMPLOYER (1) ____________________ HOW LONG ____________

ADDRESS ____________________ PHONE ____________

EMPLOYER (2) ____________________ HOW LONG ____________

ADDRESS ____________________ PHONE ____________

REFERENCES

CREDIT REFERENCES	ADDRESS	PHONE
1.		
2.		
3.		
PERSONAL REFERENCES	ADDRESS	PHONE
1.		
2.		
BANK:		

Check your work on page 54. Record your score on page 56.

ACTIVITY 2-2

YOUR GOAL: Get 8 or more points.

Read carefully the Lease Agreement that is shown on the next page. Find the answers to the following questions in the information on the Lease Agreement. Write your answer in the space provided. An example is done for you.

- The date the Lease Agreement was made is *October 19, 19--*.

1. The name of the Lessor/Landlord is ________________________.
2. The name of the Lessee/Tenant is ________________________.
3. Theresa Thomas will be renting the house located at ____.
4. This lease begins the ____________________ day of ____________________, 19—.
5. If Teresa wants to sublet the premises, she must have the prior ____ of the Landlord.
6. What utilities are furnished by the Landlord? ____
7. Who has the responsibility of mowing the lawn? ____________________.
8. Lessee agrees to keep the premises in a ____________________ and ______________________________ condition.
9. The rent is $_________________ per month.
10. The rent must be paid on the ______________________ day of each month.
11. The Security Deposit was paid in the amount of $ ____________________.
12. The lease ends the _________________ day of ____________________, 19—.

RESIDENTIAL LEASE AGREEMENT

AND SECURITY DEPOSIT RECEIPT

THIS INDENTURE, made this 29th day of October, 19 --, between Brendan Martin, hereinafter designated the Lessor or Landlord, and Teresa Thomas, hereinafter designated the Lessee,

WITNESSETH: That the said Lessor/Landlord does by these presents lease and demise the residence situated at 614 Dundas Street in Cincinnati City, Hamilton County, Ohio State, of which the real estate is described as follows:

614 Dundas Street, Cincinnati, Ohio,

upon the following terms and conditions:

1. **Term:** The premises are leased for a term of one (1) years, commencing the 1st day of November, 19 --, and terminating the 31st day of October 19 --.

2. **Rent:** The Lessee shall pay rent in the amount of $ 400.00 per month for the above premises on the 1st day of each month in advance to Landlord.

3. **Utilities:** Lessee shall pay for service and utilities supplied to the premises, except None which will be furnished by Landlord.

4. **Sublet:** The Lessee agrees not to sublet said premises nor to assign this agreement nor any part thereof without the prior written consent of Landlord.

5. **Inspection of Premises:** Lessee agrees that he has made inspection of the premises and accepts the condition of the premises in its present state, and that there are no repairs, changes, or modifications to said premises to be made by Landlord other than as listed herein.

6. **Lessee Agrees:**

(1) To keep said premises in a clean and sanitary condition;

(2) To properly dispose of rubbish, garbage and waste in a clean and sanitary manner at reasonable and regular intervals and to assume all costs of extermination and fumigation for infestation caused by Lessee;

(3) To properly use and operate all electrical, gas, heating, plumbing facilities, fixtures and appliances;

(4) To not intentionally or negligently destroy, deface, damage, impair or remove any part of the premises, their appurtenances, facilities, equipment, furniture, furnishings, and appliances, nor to permit any member of his family, invitee, licensee or other person acting under his control to do so;

(5) Not to permit a nuisance or common waste.

7. **Maintenance of Premises:** Lessee agrees to mow and water the grass and lawn, and keep the grass, lawn, flowers and shrubbery thereon in good order and condition, and keep the sidewalk surrounding said premises free and clear of all obstructions; to replace in a neat and workmanlike manner all glass and doors broken during occupancy thereof; to use due precaution against freezing of water or waste pipes and stoppage of same in and about said premises and that in case water or waste pipes are frozen or become clogged by reason of neglect of Lessee, the Lessee shall repair the same at his own expense as well as all damage caused thereby.

8. **Alterations:** Lessee agrees not to make alterations or do or cause to be done any painting or wallpapering to said premises without the prior written consent of Landlord.

9. **Use of Premises:** Lessee shall not use said premises for any purpose other than that of residence and shall not use said premises or any part thereof for ant illegal purpose. Lessee agrees to conform to municipal, county and state code, statutes, ordinances and regulations concerning the use and occupation of said premises.

10. **Pets and Animals:** Lessee shall not maintain any pets or animals upon the premises without the prior written consent of Landlord.

11. **Access:** Landlord shall have the right to place and maintain "for rent" signs in a conspicuous place on said premises for thirty days prior to the vacation of said premises. Landlord reserves the right of access to the premises for the purpose of:

(a) Inspection;

(b) Repairs, alterations or improvements;

(c) To supply services of; or

(d) To exhibit or display the premises to prospective or actual purchasers, mortgagees, tenants, workman, or contractors.

Access shall be at reasonable times except in case of emergency or abandonment.

12. **Surrender of Premises:** In the event of default in payment of any installation of rent or at the expiration of said term of this lease, Lessee will quit and surrender the said premises to Landlord.

13. **Security Deposit:** The Lessee has deposited the sum of $ 400.00 receipt of which is hereby acknowledged, which sum shall be deposited by Landlord in a trust account with Citizens bank; savings and loan association or licensed escrow, Cincinnati branch, whose address is 201 Main Street, Cincinnati, Ohio.

All or a portion of such deposit may be retained by Landlord and a refund of any portion of such deposit is conditioned as follows:

(1) Lessee shall fully perform obligations hereunder and those pursuant to Chapter 207, Laws of 1973, 1st Ex Session or as may be subsequently amended;

(2) Lessee shall occupy said premises for one (1) months or longer from date hereof;

(3) Lessee shall clean and restore said residence and return the same to Landlord in its initial condition, except for reasonable wear and tear, upon the termination of this tenancy and vacation of apartment;

(4) Lessee shall have remedied or repaired any damage to apartment premises;

(5) Lessee shall surrender to Landlord the keys to premises;

Any refund from security deposit, as by itemized statement shown to be due to Lessee, shall be returned to Lessee within fourteen (14) days after termination of this tenancy and vacation of the premises.

IN WITNESS WHEREOF, the Lessee has hereunto set his hand and seal the day and year first above written.

Brendan Martin	Teresa Thomas
LANDLORD	LESSEE

601 Dundas Street

Cincinnati, Ohio

ADDRESS

☞ ***Check your work on page 54. Record your score on page 56.***

UNIT 3 Buying Transportation

WHAT YOU WILL LEARN

When you finish this unit, you will be able to:

- List three basic transportation choices.
- Identify six terms commonly used in buying and selling automobiles.
- List four cost considerations involved in owning a car.
- List four sources of used cars.
- List ten things to check before buying a used car.
- List six steps to follow in buying a used car.
- List three things to consider in buying a new car.
- List six steps to follow in buying a new car.

Tony and Rose Anna Valentine were thinking of buying a car. Several things made them think that might be a good idea. Tony's coworker Brad had offered to pay for rides to work. Rose Anna's hours were now the same as Tony's, so they could also save her bus fare. Tony thought car payments might not be much more than the amount they were spending on bus fares. Rose Anna knew they would also enjoy the convenience of having their own car.

Tony and Rose Anna began to consider their transportation choices. In this unit, you and the Valentines will learn about buying transportation.

TRANSPORTATION CHOICES

An automobile is one of the most expensive purchases most people make. But there are many other transportation choices.

Everyone has different transportation needs, too. Before considering their choices, Tony and Rose Anna decided to look closely at their needs and costs. To find out what they were spending, they made a list of all their trips for one month and the transportation cost for each trip. Then they multiplied the transportation cost by the number of trips taken. Their list of monthly transportation costs is shown here, in Illustration 3-1.

		Cost Per Round Trip			
Destination	Number of Round Trips Per Month	Bus/ Train/ Subway	Cab	Other	Total Per Month
Job(s):					
Rose Anna's	20	$ 1.50	$	$	$ 30.00
Tony's	20	1.50			30.00
School:					
Adult Ed. Class (carpool)	8			2.00	16.00
Day Care (Bus—Buster)	20	1.00			20.00
Shopping:					
Grocery	8	1.00			8.00
Mall	4	2.00			8.00
Meetings:					
PTA (carpool)	1			2.00	2.00
Church (2 adults)	4	2.50			10.00
Entertainment:					
Visit Friends/ Relatives	6	3.00			18.00
Movies, Sports, etc.	4	2.50			10.00
Other:					
Occasional Cab	3		6.00		18.00
Misc. — Doctor/ Dentist	6		3.00		18.00
Total Monthly Transportation Costs					$188.00

Illustration 3-1

Tony and Rose Anna's Monthly Transportation Costs

Illustration 3-2

An automobile is one of the most expensive purchases most people make.

Once they knew their monthly transportation needs and costs, Tony and Rose Anna began to look at their choices. The choices they considered were walking and bicycling, public transportation, taxicabs, carpool, and owning a car.

Walking and Bicycling

Walking and bicycling are the two cheapest forms of transportation available. They are also the healthiest. If you can allow an extra thirty minutes to walk or bicycle on short trips, you can save money. Weather problems must be considered when you walk or bicycle. But the extra benefits of good health and dollars saved can make these good transportation choices.

Public Transportation

Bus and rail facilities are available in most large towns and cities. Learn the routes followed by these services. A combination of short walks with public transportation is a common choice.

Taxicabs

Taking a taxi is one of the most expensive transportation choices. Sometimes a taxi is the only choice available. Tony and Rose Anna had to take a taxi to visit his mother in a nearby nursing home. They knew these trips would become more frequent. When you are having to use taxis often, it is a good time to consider buying a car.

Carpool

A **carpool** is an arrangement in which several people ride with the owner of a car. Carpooling saves money for the owner because the riders share expenses. Carpooling saves money for the riders because they have transportation they need without having to buy a car. Disadvantages occur when the driver is late, or when any member of the carpool is unreliable.

Owning a Car

Owning a car is one of the most expensive transportation choices. Many people enjoy the convenience of a car, though. In rural areas and many towns and cities, owning a car is almost a necessity due to lack of public transportation. In some major cities, it is not desirable to own a car. Traffic, parking shortages, and high insurance costs make owning a car undesirable in cities like New York, Chicago, and Los Angeles. Owning a car also means more costs than just the monthly payments.

CHECKPOINT 3-1

YOUR GOAL: Get 4 or more points.

Read carefully the statements below. Each statement is either true or false. Write *T* (true) or *F* (false) beside each statement in the space provided. An example is done for you.

__*T*__ • Bicycling is one of the cheapest forms transportation.

______ 1. Parking shortages can make car ownership undesirable in a crowded city.

______ 2. Buses usually cost more than taxicabs.

______ 3. Carpools save money because riders share expenses.

______ 4. Owning a car is one of the more expensive transportation choices.

______ 5. Public transportation will always take you where you want to go.

☞ ***Check your work on page 54. Record your score on page 56.***

Terms Used in Buying and Selling Cars

Tony and Rose Anna started looking at cars. It seemed like the dealers spoke another language! If you understand that language, you can avoid making mistakes when buying and selling cars. Some of the terms most commonly used include the following:

- **Bait and switch**. A sales tactic with which you are attracted by an ad for one car, and the salesperson then tries to sell you another usually more expensive one.
- **Book Value**. The value of a car listed in one of several official guide books. The most common of these books is published by the National Automobile Dealers Association (NADA).
- **Dealer's cost**. The price the auto dealer pays the manufacturer for a new car.
- **Dealer's preparation charge.** The price charged by a dealer to get a new car in running condition (oil, gas, etc.). Also called *dealer prep*.
- **Demonstrator (demo).** A car used by sales personnel and potential customers for test driving.
- **Depreciation.** The yearly decline in an automobile's value.
- **Disclaimer.** A written or verbal statement that the dealer is not responsible for a certain circumstance or condition.
- **Express warranty**. A written agreement that spells out responsibilities of the buyer and seller.
- **Full warranty.** A written agreement that a defective part will be repaired or replaced at no charge.
- **Implied warranty.** An unwritten agreement that exists with a sale. For instance, if you buy a car right after the salesperson has driven you around the block in it, there is an implied warranty that the car is in running order.
- **Limited warranty.** A written agreement that a defective product will be repaired or replaced only under certain conditions. For instance, a limited warranty may say a part will be replaced if it breaks, but you will be charged for the labor.
- **Odometer.** Indicator showing how many miles an automobile has been driven. In most states it is against the law to tamper with the odometer of a car. If you suspect that the odometer has been rolled back to show fewer miles driven, you should walk away.
- **Options.** Extra items that a buyer may or may not purchase with a car.
- **Repossessed automobile (Repo).** An automobile taken back by a bank or finance agency because the buyer failed to make payments.

- **Sticker price.** The manufacturer's suggested retail price for a new automobile shown on the window sticker.

THE COSTS OF OWNING AN AUTOMOBILE

Tony and Rose Anna knew what they were already spending on transportation. Tony thought they should buy a car. "I saw an ad for a car at Metro Motors," he said. "Payments are just $140 a month." Rose Anna answered, "Payments are just one part of the cost. We must plan for other costs, too. We should also compare new car costs with used car options." Some of the costs of car ownership Tony and Rose Anna considered are financing, gas and oil, insurance, licenses, parking, and taxes.

Finance Costs

Finance costs can affect your monthly payments. **Finance costs** are the charges a finance agency makes in return for allowing you to drive an automobile while you are still paying for it. Finance costs are added to the purchase price you pay. Always get the total finance costs (interest rate and other charges) in writing before you sign a sales agreement.

Gas, Oil, and Maintenance

Gas and oil will be weekly expenses. Because these costs vary from week to week, your budget should plan for increases. Repair and maintenance costs should be included in your budget. With a new car, you may choose to buy a service agreement so that most of these costs are paid for by the dealer. For a used car, you can expect to spend between $500 and $1,000 on repair and maintenance the first year of ownership.

Insurance

Insurance can cost even more than the car itself. Insurance costs vary widely. You will pay more for insurance if you live in a major city, if you have teenage drivers in the family, or if you live in a high crime area. Expect to pay a minimum of between $400 and $600 a year for insurance.

Licenses, Parking, and Taxes

Other costs will include driver's license, license tags, tolls and parking, and taxes. If you do not have parking provided at work or if you must use toll roads or bridges, parking and toll fees will also increase costs of car ownership.

Tony and Rose Anna made a list of everything that would add to the cost of owning a car. Their list is shown next, in Illustration 3-3.

Expense	One Month	One Year
Monthly Payment	$140	$1,680
Insurance	20	240
Gas	50	600
Oil Changes. Lubrication, Tune-ups	15	180
Repairs, Parts and Labor, Replacement of Tires and Batteries	50	600
Tolls	5	60
Parking	5	60
Licenses	5	60
Total	$290	$3,480

Illustration 3-3

Rose Anna and Tony's Car Ownership Expenses

CHECKPOINT 3-2

YOUR GOAL: Get 6 or more points.

Read carefully the following statements. Complete each statement by filling in a word or words in the space provided. Use words from the list that follows the last statement on the next page. An example is done for you.

- Car insurance will cost more if you live in a _high crime_ area.

1. It is usually possible to reduce repair and maintenance costs for a new car by purchasing a ________________.
2. ________________ are charges made by the finance agency in return for allowing you to drive a car while you are paying for it.

3. Insurance costs will be at least ____________________ a year.

4. ________________________ are regular costs of driving a car.

5. Finance costs include ____________________ and fees charged.

6. A ________________________ is a written agreement that a defective part will be repaired or replaced at no charge.

7. The __________________________ shows how many miles an automobile has been driven.

8. A car used by sales personnel and customers for test driving is called a ____________________________.

odometer
$400 to $600
gas and oil
service agreement
finance costs
full warranty
high crime
demonstrator
interest

☞ *Check your work on page 54. Record your score on page 56.*

BUYING A USED AUTOMOBILE

A used car can be a good source of transportation. A used car can also cause you trouble. Make sure you look carefully before you buy, and use every chance to lower your risk.

Sources of Used Cars

One way to lower your risk in buying a new car is to check into as many sources as possible. Among these sources are new and used car dealers, private sellers, car rental agencies, and repossessed cars.

New Car Dealers

Most new car dealers resell the cars they take in on trades. You can often get limited warranties or service agreements on used cars purchased through major new car dealers.

Used Car Dealers

Used car dealers often have good selections. You should try to work with used car dealers you know about. Ask your friends about dealers who are honest and reliable. Know what is and is not warranted.

Private Sellers

If you know cars very well, private sellers can be your best source for a used car. Private sellers are not businesses and do not have to make a profit, which would add to the cost of the car. If you buy from a private seller, be sure you know the book value of the car. Remember that there are no warranties given when you buy from a private seller.

Car Rental Agencies

Car rental agencies usually sell their cars when the mileage is still fairly low. They can be good sources for used cars because they often do not have to show a very high profit on used cars they sell. There are usually no warranties given on these cars.

Repossessed Cars

Banks and finance agencies sell used cars that they take back if the buyer fails to make payments. Sometimes these are very low mileage cars. Like rental agency used cars, though, you have no way of knowing how the car was used. There are usually no warranties given with repossessed cars.

Things to Check before Buying a Used Car

Before you buy a used car, find out the book value. You can ask any bank or finance company loan officer for this information. Give the loan officer the make and year of the car. If the car is in very good condition, has low mileage, or has options like stereo or power windows, it will be worth a little more than book value. If it is in very poor condition, it will be worth less.

Always test drive a used car before you buy it. Have a mechanic who is not involved with the sale check the car before you buy it.

There are other things that can help you avoid mistakes when buying a used car. Look for these possible trouble spots:

1. *Car body*. Avoid cars with rust spots. Rust can grow very quickly. Broken or cracked glass or dents in the car can indicate that it has been wrecked or not well cared for.

2. *Motor*. Check, or ask a mechanic to check, for cracks in the block. See that all major engine parts are in good condition.
3. *Brakes and wheels*. If the car pulls in one direction, its tires may be bad or the wheels out of alignment. **Alignment** is the arrangement of the car in a straight line or in proper position. If a car is out of alignment, it will not drive properly.
4. *Systems*. Check, or have a mechanic check, to make sure the electrical, cooling, and lighting systems are all working well and do not have leaks or defects.
5. *Options*. If you are buying a used car with options like air conditioning, rear window defroster, or special features that are important to you, make sure these features are working properly.

Guidelines for Buying a Used Car

In addition to checking for trouble spots, following guidelines can also help you avoid mistakes. These guidelines include:

1. Choose your dealer carefully.
2. Compare the car you are buying with its book value.
3. Choose a recent car model so that replacement parts will not be hard to find.
4. Take your time.
5. Avoid sales pitches or other attempts to rush you.
6. Always test drive the car.

CHECKPOINT 3-3

YOUR GOAL: Get 5 or more points.

Read carefully the statements below. Each statement is either true or false. Write *T* (true) or *F* (false) beside each statement in the space provided. An example is done for you.

T • New car dealers can be good sources of used cars.

_____ 1. It is a good idea to pay more than the book value of a used car if it is in fair condition.

_____ 2. Rust spots can cause trouble on a car.

_____ 3. If a car pulls in one direction, that may mean the car is out of alignment.

_____ 4. Car rental agencies do not sell their rental cars unless they have been wrecked.

______ 5. Options, such as stereo or power windows, can increase the value of a car.

______ 6. Recent models are generally better used car buys than very old models.

☞ ***Check your work on page 54. Record your score on page 56.***

MAKING YOUR MONEY WORK FOR YOU

There are state and federal agencies to help you make wise transportation choices. Most have books with up-to-date tips. Look in your telephone book for the State Department of Transportation or Department of Motor Vehicles. You can also call or write the Federal Trade Commission, Office of the Secretary, Washington, D.C. 20580 (phone 202-523-3600) for free booklets.

BUYING A NEW AUTOMOBILE

New cars are often good transportation choices. They have the advantage of warranties and the latest improvements. Be sure you consider things important to you and follow guidelines for buying a new car.

Things to Consider When Buying a New Car

Many items need to be checked and compared when buying a new car as when buying a used car.

1. *Price*. Know the maximum amount you can pay. Buy a car for that amount or less. Don't consider just the monthly payment. Dealers may try to get you to buy a higher priced car by suggesting a longer payment period. Remember that the longer the payment period, the higher your total cost.
2. *Options*. Air conditioners, radios, cassette or CD players, special wheel covers, tilt steering wheel, and other items add to the total cost.
3. *Dealer*. Ask your friends and family about their experiences with cars and dealers. Do business with dealers that have a reputation for being fair and honest.
4. *Timing*. Shop when prices are lower. The late summer, just before the new models come out, is usually the time of lowest prices. New cars from previous years that haven't sold will be marked down, also.
5. *Shopping*. Take time to compare different cars and different dealers. One dealer may offer the same car and model at a

lower price. Don't be fooled by gimmicks such as prizes for buying only on a certain day or for buying a certain car.

Guidelines for Buying a New Car

Don't be in a hurry to buy your new car. Following these guidelines can also help you make the right decision.

1. *Check the sticker price.* This will be on the car window. Make sure you are not buying a car with options that are not important to you.
2. *Test drive the car.* Ask about anything that does not feel or sound exactly as it should.
3. *Don't be afraid to bargain.* Ask for the minimum price that the dealer will accept. Don't be afraid to make an offer lower than the price advertised.
4. *Ask about discounts or rebates.* Some discounts or rebates are available only to those who ask about them.
5. *Review all warranties.* Make sure these are in writing. Keep them in a safe place when you purchase the car.
6. *Get written copies of all sales agreements.* If you are promised something, such as a free oil change, get it in writing.
7. *Ask about the dealer's acceptance of trade-ins.* Write down what you are told.
8. *Don't be afraid to get other opinions.* Take a friend with you to look at the car and listen to what the salesperson tells you.

CHECKPOINT 3-4

YOUR GOAL: Get 4 or more points.

Read carefully the following statements. Complete each statement by filling in the space provided. Use words from the list that follows the statements. An example is done for you.

- The sticker price of a new car will list *optional* equipment.

1. New car prices are usually lower in ____________________.
2. It is important to get ____________________ copies of warranties and agreements.
3. Before buying a new car, ask about ____________________ and ____________________.

4. A dealer should tell you about acceptance of ______________________________.

5. You should visit ______________________________ dealers before making a decision on a new car.

discounts
rebates
several
trade-ins
optional
late summer
written

☞ ***Check your work on page 54. Record your score on page 56.***

WHAT YOU HAVE LEARNED

After studying this unit you have learned:

- Three basic transportation choices.
- Terms commonly used in buying and selling automobiles.
- Four cost considerations involved in owning a car.
- Four sources of used cars.
- Ten things to check before buying a used car.
- Guidelines for buying a used car.
- Three things to consider in buying a new car.
- Guidelines for buying a new car.

PUTTING IT TOGETHER

ACTIVITY 3-1

YOUR GOAL: Get 5 or more points.

Determine the cost of your family's transportation. Assume that you use public transportation for everything. Include trips for all members of your family. Write in the space provided the destination for each trip, the number of round trips to that destination made each month, and the cost of each round trip. Multiply the number of trips by the cost per round trip to get the total cost for that trip per month. Add the monthly totals to get the grand total of monthly transportation costs.

Destination	Number of Round Trips Per Month	Cost Per Round Trip: Bus/ Train/ Subway	Cost Per Round Trip: Cab	Cost Per Round Trip: Other	Total Per Month
Job(s):					
______	______	$_____	$_____	$_____	$______
______	______	_____	_____	_____	______
School:					
______	______	_____	_____	_____	______
______	______	_____	_____	_____	______
Shopping:					
______	______	_____	_____	_____	______
______	______	_____	_____	_____	______
Meetings:					
______	______	_____	_____	_____	______
______	______	_____	_____	_____	______
Entertainment:					
______	______	_____	_____	_____	______
______	______	_____	_____	_____	______
Other:					
______	______	_____	_____	_____	______
______	______	_____	_____	_____	______
TOTAL MONTHLY TRANSPORTATION COSTS ...					$______

☞ *Check your work on page 54. Record your score on page 56.*

ACTIVITY 3-2 YOUR GOAL: Get 5 or more points

Determine the *monthly* costs of owning a car for your family. Choose a car from the ads shown below. Figure the cost of each item as directed below. Suggestions for ways to determine the cost are given with each item.

1988 4-Dr Sedan
Air, 30,000 miles
Was $6995
Now **$5688**

1991 2-Dr Coupe
Air, low miles
Was $11,945
Now $9988

1988 Sport Truck
5 spd., air,
Only 21,000 miles
Was $4995
Now $3488

BRAND NEW SPORTSTER
$11,988
Several to choose from! Air conditioning, V-8 engine, overdrive trans., driver's air bag, AM/FM stereo with cass. player, 18" wheels, power steering and brakes.

MONTHLY PAYMENT (including financing costs) .... $________
Call a bank, finance company, or car dealer and ask what the monthly payment would be for the price of the car you want. (Example: To finance $9,000 at 11-1/2% interest costs $198 a month for 5 years.)

INSURANCE .... $________
Call an insurance agent and ask for the monthly cost of the minimum recommended insurance for your state.

GAS .... $________
Assume that you will drive 1,000 miles a month and your car will get 20 miles per gallon of gas. You will buy approximately 50 gallons of gas a month. Find out the cost of one gallon of gas; multiply by 50.

OIL CHANGES, LUBRICATION, TUNE-UPS .... $________
Ask a local mechanic for an estimate on the car you chose. If you cannot get an estimate, use an average of $15 a month.

REPAIRS, PARTS AND LABOR, INCLUDING REPLACEMENT OF TIRES AND BATTERIES .... $________
These costs are very low for the first year or two for a new car. For a used car, you will spend an average of $40 to $80 a month, depending on the age and condition of the car.

TOLLS .... $________
Do you regularly drive on highways, bridges, or tunnels which require the payment of a toll? If so, figure the monthly cost.

PARKING .... $________
Must you pay for parking while you are at work or at home on a regular basis? Add in occasional parking charges for downtown garages/meters.

LICENSES AND TAGS .... $________
Divide the amount for licenses/tags in your state by 12.

TOTAL .... $________

☞ ***Check your work on page 54. Record your score on page 56.***

CHECKING WHAT YOU LEARNED

Now you can see how much you have learned about making major financial decisions. These 20 questions cover the main topics you studied in this book. There is no time limit, so take your time.

After you finish, check your answers. Give yourself 1 point for each correct answer. Record your score on your Personal Progress Record. The evaluation chart will tell you where you may need additional study.

DIRECTIONS: Each statement is either true or false. Write *T* (true) or *F* (false) in the space provided.

______ 1. Credit allows you to buy an item when you need it but do not have the cash.

______ 2. You can be denied credit just because you are not married.

______ 3. You are using credit wisely when you pay for dinner with a credit card.

______ 4. A good use of credit is purchasing a major appliance.

______ 5. Everyone has a right to a credit card.

______ 6. There is no cost of credit charged to the consumer.

______ 7. You should never sign a blank loan or installment contract.

______ 8. A townhouse is a small apartment located in the downtown area.

______ 9. The landlord is the person owning the house or apartment for rent.

______ 10. The lease is an agreement that is important only to the landlord.

______ 11. The legal proceeding by which a landlord can force a tenant to move is called a *forfeiture.*

______ 12. When looking for housing, location is very important.

______ 13. The landlord is responsible for extermination of rats and mice.

______ 14. Tenants must make all major plumbing repairs.

______ 15. You will need both credit references and personal references when completing a rental application.

______ 16. A combination of short walks with public transportation is the most common transportation choice.

______ 17. Taking a taxicab is the least expensive method of transportation.

______ 18. Traffic and high insurance rates make owning a car undesirable in many crowded cities.

______ 19. It is important to get written copies of warranties and agreements.

______ 20. Car rental agencies sell their cars only if they are damaged.

Check your work on page 54. Record your score on page 57.

GLOSSARY

A

After-tax income. Take-home pay after social security and income tax are deducted.

Alignment. The arrangement of a car in a straight line or in proper position.

B

Bait and switch. A sales tactic with which you are attracted by an ad for one car, and the salesperson then tries to sell you another.

Bank card. A credit agreement through which you can continue to charge purchases even though you have not paid the account in full.

Book value. The value of a car listed in one of several official guide books.

C

Carpool. An arrangement in which several people share the use of a car.

Charge account. Credit for merchandise given by a store.

Contract. An agreement between two parties.

Cosign. To promise to repay a loan if the borrower does not.

Credit. Buying something now and agreeing to pay for it later; borrowing money now and agreeing to pay it back later.

D

Dealer's cost. The price the auto dealer pays the manufacturer for a new car.

Dealer's preparation charge. The price charged by a dealer to get a new car in running condition. Also called *dealer prep*.

Demonstrator (demo). A car used by sales personnel and customers for test driving.

Depreciation. The yearly decline in an automobile's value.

Disclaimer. A written or verbal statement that the dealer is not responsible for a certain circumstance or condition.

Discrimination. The act of showing different favor or treatment on the basis of reasons other than individual merit.

Duplex. A two-family home.

E

Efficiency apartment. A small apartment consisting of one large room that serves as kitchen, living room and bedroom.

Eviction. Legal proceeding by which a landlord can force a tenant to move out.

Express warranty. A written agreement that spells out responsibilities of the buyer and seller.

F

Finance costs. The charges a finance company makes in return for allowing you to drive an automobile while you are still paying for it.

Forfeiture. Giving up your security deposit when you fail to meet obligations of the lease.

Full warranty. A written agreement that a defective part will be repaired or replaced at no charge.

H

House. A single-family home separate from other dwellings.

Housing authority. City or county agency set up to uphold building and housing codes.

I

Implied warranty. An unwritten agreement that exists with a sale.

Installment loan. A contract in which the total purchase price and credit cost is divided into equal amounts for repayments.

Interest. The amount your money will earn. The amount paid for the use of capital.

L

Landlord. The person owning the house or apartment you rent. Also called *lessor*.

Lay-away. A plan allowing consumers to put aside an item until it is paid for in full.

Lease. A legal agreement between landlord and tenant listing all obligations and requirements of occupancy.

Lessee. Person renting the house or apartment. Also called *tenant*.

Lessor. Person owning the house or apartment you rent. Also called *landlord*.

Limited warranty. A written agreement that a defective product will be repaired or replaced only under certain conditions.

O

Odometer. Mileage indicator showing how many miles an automobile has been driven.

Options. Extra items that a buyer may or may not purchase with a car.

P

Pawnshop. A shop that lends money in exchange for personal property left to the shop. If the loan is not repaid, the borrower forfeits the property.

R

Rent. Payment for use of property.

Repossessed automobile (repo). A car taken back by a bank or finance agency because the buyer failed to make payments.

Risk. The chance the lender takes as to whether or not the borrower will pay what is owed.

S

Security deposit. Money deposited by a tenant in advance on a rental agreement and held as security against any damage that may be caused by the tenant.

Sticker price. The manufacturer's suggested retail price for a new automobile shown on the window sticker.

Sublet. To rent your house or apartment to someone else while you continue to pay the landlord.

T

Tenant. Person renting the house or apartment. Also called *lessee*.

Townhouse. A large apartment, usually two-story, with separate living and dining areas.

INDEX

ANSWERS

✔ CHECKING WHAT YOU KNOW

1. **T**
2. **T**
3. **F**
4. **F**
5. **T**
6. **T**
7. **F**
8. **T**
9. **F**
10. **T**
11. **F**
12. **T**
13. **F**
14. **T**
15. **F**
16. **T**
17. **F**
18. **T**
19. **T**
20. **T**

UNIT 1

CHECKPOINT 1-1, page 4

Give yourself 1 point for each correct answer.

1. **groceries, gas**
2. **credit**
3. **permanent residence**
4. **credit risk**
5. **car, home**

CHECKPOINT 1-2, page 6

Give yourself 1 point for each correct answer.

1. **T**
2. **F**
3. **F**
4. **T**
5. **F**

CHECKPOINT 1-3, page 10

Give yourself 1 point for each correct answer.

1. **A**
2. **E**
3. **B**
4. **F**
5. **C**

CHECKPOINT 1-4, page 12

Give yourself 1 point for each correct answer.

1. **balance owing**
2. **landlords**
3. **name, business address**
4. **finance company**
5. **date**

ACTIVITY 1-1, page 14

Give yourself 10 points for completing the loan application. Answers will vary.

ACTIVITY 1-2, page 15

Give yourself 1 point for each correct answer.

1. **b**
2. **d**
3. **e**
4. **f**
5. **g**
6. **c**
7. **h**
8. **d**
9. **e**
10. **g**

UNIT 2

CHECKPOINT 2-1, page 19

Give yourself 1 point for each correct answer.

1. **monthly**
2. **efficiency**
3. **landlord; lessor**
4. **townhouse**
5. **housing authority**
6. **eviction**

CHECKPOINT 2-2, page 22

Give yourself 1 point for each correct answer.

1. **F**
2. **F**
3. **T**
4. **F**
5. **T**
6. **T**
7. **F**
8. **T**

CHECKPOINT 2-3, page 25

Give yourself 1 point for each correct answer.

1. **F**
2. **T**
3. **T**
4. **F**
5. **T**
6. **F**

ACTIVITY 2-1, page 28

Give yourself 5 points for completing the Rental Application. Answers will vary.

ACTIVITY 2-2, page 29

Give yourself 1 point for each correct answer.

1. **Brenda Martin**
2. **Teresa Thomas**
3. **614 Dundas Street, Cincinnati, Ohio**
4. **1st, November**
5. **written consent**
6. **none**
7. **Teresa Thomas (or Lessee/Tenant)**
8. **clean, sanitary**
9. **$400**
10. **1st**
11. **$400**
12. **31st, October**

UNIT 3

CHECKPOINT 3-1, page 34

Give yourself 1 point for each correct answer.

1. **T**
2. **F**
3. **T**
4. **T**
5. **F**

CHECKPOINT 3-2, page 37

Give yourself 1 point for each correct answer.

1. **service agreement**
2. **finance costs**
3. **$400 to $600**
4. **gas and oil**
5. **interest**
6. **full warranty**
7. **odometer**
8. **demonstrator**

CHECKPOINT 3-3, page 40

Give yourself 1 point for each correct answer.

1. **F**
2. **T**
3. **T**
4. **F**
5. **T**
6. **T**

CHECKPOINT 3-4, page 42

Give yourself 1 point for each correct answer.

1. **late summer**
2. **written**
3. **discounts, rebates**
4. **trade-ins**
5. **several**

ACTIVITY 3-1, page 44

Give yourself 1 point for each category in which you completed at least one destination and 1 point for the total.

ACTIVITY 3-2, page 45

Give yourself 1 point for each cost determined and 1 point for the total. Answers will vary.

✔ CHECKING WHAT YOU LEARNED

1. **T**
2. **F**
3. **F**
4. **T**
5. **F**
6. **F**
7. **T**
8. **T**
9. **T**
10. **F**
11. **F**
12. **T**
13. **T**
14. **F**
15. **T**
16. **F**
17. **F**
18. **T**
19. **T**
20. **F**

PERSONAL PROGRESS RECORD

Name: ______________________________

✔ CHECKING WHAT YOU KNOW

Use the chart below to determine the areas you need to do the most work. In the space provided, write the total number of points you got right for each content area. Then add up the total number of points right to find your final score. Circle those items you answered correcly. As you begin your study, pay close attention to those areas where you missed half or more of the questions.

Content Area	Item Number	Study Pages	Total Points	Number Right
UNIT 1				
Establishing Credit	1, 2,3, 4	1-7	4	
Credit Rights; Loans	5, 6, 7	8-13	3	
Unit 2				
Housing Choices	8, 9, 10	17-21	3	
Landlord and Tenant Responsibilities	11, 12, 13	21-23	3	
Rental and Lease Forms	14	23-27	1	
Unit 3				
Transportation Choices	15	31-36	1	
Costs of Car Ownership	16, 17, 18	36-38	3	
Buying a Car	19, 20	39-43	2	

Date ______________________ Total Points: 20 Your Score: ______

UNIT 1: Understanding Credit

Exercise	Score
Checkpoint 1-1	________
Checkpoint 1-2	________
Checkpoint 1-3	________
Checkpoint 1-4	________
Activity 1-1	________
Activity 1-2	________
Total	________

HOW ARE YOU DOING?

35 or better	Excellent
30-34	Good
25-29	Fair
Below 25	See Instructor

UNIT 2: Understanding Housing Choices

Exercise	Score
Checkpoint 2-1	________
Checkpoint 2-2	________
Checkpoint 2-3	________
Activity 2-1	________
Activity 2-2	________
Total	________

HOW ARE YOU DOING?

27 or better	Excellent
23-26	Good
19-22	Fair
Below 19	See Instructor

UNIT 3: Buying Transportation

Exercise	Score
Checkpoint 3-1	________
Checkpoint 3-2	________
Checkpoint 3-3	________
Checkpoint 3-4	________
Activity 3-1	________
Activity 3-2	________
Total	________

HOW ARE YOU DOING?

30 or better	Excellent
27-29	Good
24-26	Fair
Below 24	See Instructor

Name: ______________________________

CHECKING WHAT YOU LEARNED

Use the chart below to determine the areas you need to do the most review. In the space provided, write the total number of points you got right for each content area. Review those areas where you missed half or more of the questions. Then add up the total number of points right to find your final score.

Content Area	Item Number	Study Pages	Total Points	Number Right
UNIT 1				
Establishing Credit	1, 3, 4, 6	1, 3, 4, 6, 7	4	
Credit Rights and Loans	2, 5, 7	8-13	3	
Unit 2				
Housing Choices	8, 12	17-21	2	
Landlord and Tenant Responsibilities	9, 11, 13, 14	21-23	4	
Rental and Lease Forms	10, 15	23-27	2	
Unit 3				
Transportation Choices	16, 17	31-36	2	
Costs of Car Ownership	18	36-38	1	
Buying a Car	19, 20	39-43	2	

Date ______________________ Total Points: 20 Your Score: ______